Samsung Galaxy A15 5G User Manual For Seniors

A Comprehensive Step by Step Manual on How to Use and Master Galaxy A15 with Screenshots, and Updated Tips and Tricks For Setup, Configuration and Usage

Jazz K. Famous

Table of Contents

Introduction

Samsung Galaxy A15 User Guide Introduction
Modern smartphones like the Samsung Galaxy A15 are made to be simple to use and seamless for consumers. It's crucial to know how to use and maximize your Phone given its amazing features and capabilities. This user guide covers a wide range of topics, including [1]: giving you a thorough overview of the Samsung Galaxy A15.

- **Activation and Setup***: Discover how to transfer files from your old device and set up your new one, as well as how to activate and set up your Samsung Galaxy A15.

- ***Device Tutorial***: Learn how to use your Samsung Galaxy A15 with interactive instructions, along with helpful hints to improve your experience.

- ***Top Features and Functions***: Learn how to make use of key features like notification management, screen lock, and camera settings.

- ***Troubleshooting***: Discover fixes for typical difficulties, such restarting your gadget, clearing the preferences for apps, and fixing connectivity issues.

- ***Tips & Tricks***: Make the most of your Samsung Galaxy A15 by following professional tips on productivity, customization, and other topics.

Chapter One
Turn on device

Make use of the side button in order to activate the device. It is not advisable to make use of the device in a damaged or fractured state. Utilize the device immediately following its repair.

- o Press and hold the side key to activate the device.

- To power down the device, simultaneously press and hold the Side and Volume buttons before selecting ⏻ Power off. Give your consent when prompted.

- To restart the device, simultaneously press and hold the Side and Volume buttons before selecting ⏻ Restart. After that, give your approval when prompted.

Note: For optimal 5G performance, a robust 5G connection and unobstructed antennas (located on the rear of the device) are required. For information on network availability, please contact the service providers. Additionally, coverage or a case may impede 5G performance.

Use the setup wizard

When you first power on your device, the Setup Wizard guides you through the fundamentals of device configuration.

To select the default language, connect to a Wi-Fi network, configure accounts, enable location services, and gain access to additional device information, simply adhere to the on-screen prompts.

Transfer data from old device

To transfer media from the old device, including photos, contacts, videos, audio, messages, calendars, and notes, it is recommended that you download the Smart Switch. The Smart Switch supports data transfer via USB cable, computer, and Wi-Fi.

1. Select Accounts & backup > Transfer data from the old device from the Settings menu.

2. Follow the instructions and select the items to be transferred.

Lock or unlock your device

Apply security to your device by utilizing its screen lock function. Your device locks automatically when the screen times out by default.

Side key/Fingerprint scanner
Press to lock.
Press to turn on the screen, and then swipe the screen to unlock it.

Side button settings

Customizable shortcuts are those that are designated to the Side key.

Click twice

Determine which feature is initiated when the Side button is double-tapped.

1. Select   Advanced features from the Settings menu, then press the Side key.

2. To activate this function, double-press the contact pad and select the following options:

- By default, quick launch cameras
- Launch the application

Press and hold

Determine which feature is activated when the Side key is pressed and held down.

1. Select   Advanced features from the Settings menu, followed by the Side key.

2. In the Press & Hold heading, select the following options:

- Bixby (the default) wakes up
- Power-off menus are included.

Accounts

Manage and configure the accounts.

Note: Accounts may provide access to email, calendars, contacts, and additional functionalities.

Creating a Google Account

To access Google Cloud Storage, applications installed directly from the account, and to fully utilize the Android™ features on your device, please log in to your Google Account.

After establishing a lock screen and logging into your Google Account, Google Devices Protection is activated. The data associated with your Google Account is required for this service to perform a factory settings reset.

1. Select Manage accounts from the 🔄 Accounts & backup menu in the Settings menu.

2. Select ✛ "Add account" followed by "Google."

Add Samsung account

To gain comprehensive access to Samsung applications and exclusive access to Samsung content, please log in to your Samsung account.

o In the Settings menu, select Samsung account.

Add Outlook profile

Access your Outlook® account through a login in order to view and manage your email correspondence.

1. Select Manage accounts from the Accounts & backup menu in the Settings menu.

2. Select Add account, followed by Outlook.

Set up voicemail

When you first access voicemail service, you have the ability to configure it. Voicemail can be accessed through the Phone application.

1. Touch or hold down one key while on the phone to access the voicemail.

2. Generate a password, record greetings, and enter your own name by adhering to the tutorial.

Navigation

The touch screen responds most effectively to mild pressure applied with a capacitive stylus or finger pad. Applying excessive force or metallic objects to a touch screen may result in surface damage that is not covered by the warranty.

Touch

To select or uncover an item, a light touch is required.

- To select an item, simply touch it.

- One can zoom in or out of an image by performing a double-tap.

Swipe

It is recommended to delicately drag your finger across the screen.

- Swipe the display to activate the device.
- To navigate the Home screens or menu options, use the swipe gesture on your screen.

Drop and drag

Tap and hold the item, then drag it to a new location.

- To add an application shortcut to the Home screen, simply drag it into place.
- By dragging a widget to a different location, it is possible to relocate it.

Zooming in and out

To zoom in and out, place your forefinger and thumb on the display alternatively, either together or separately.

- To perform a simple zoom in, position your forefinger and thumb at an appropriate distance from the screen.

- To execute a simple zoom out, align your forefinger and fingertip on the display.

Press and hold

By touching and holding an item, it is possible to activate it.

- Touch and hold the field to display the option pop-up menus.
- Customization of the Home screen is possible by touching and holding the screen.

Navigation bar

You have the option of using the full-screen gestures or the navigation keys to navigate your device.

Recent apps ——————— ||| O   < ——————— Back

Home

Navigation key

Utilize the navigation controls located at the bottom of the screen for quick access.

1. Tap Display in the Settings menu, then select Navigation bar, followed by Buttons.

2. Select the option beneath the Button order to determine which displays' sides the Back and Recent applications icons will appear on.

Navigation gestures

Conceal your navigation controls at the screen's base to provide a clear viewing experience. Swipe actionably to navigate the device instead.

1. To enable the gesture feature, navigate to Settings > Select Display > Tap Navigation bar > Swipe touch.

2. To modify settings, touch:

   From the Additional options, choose gesture type and sensitivity.

   • Gesture hints: Display lines at the bottom of the screen that indicate the location of all screen gestures.

   – Change applications while hints are hidden: If this option has been enabled, you can still transition between applications using the gesture even after the gesture hint has been disabled.

- The ability to hide the keyboard is indicated by an icon in the lower right corner of the screen when the device is in portrait mode.

Customize home screen

The device's home screen serves as the initial site of navigation. In addition to organizing your preferred applications and widgets, you can establish additional Home screens, delete screens, rearrange the order of the screens, and choose the primary Home screen from this menu.

Application icon

In order to launch an application from any of the Home displays, utilize the application icon.

o Touch and hold an application icon from the Applications menu, then tap Add to Home.

To eliminate an icon:

o Select Remove by holding down an application icon directly from the Home screen.

Note: Deleting icons from the Home screen does not eliminate the application; it merely removes the icon.

Wallpaper

To modify the visual aesthetics of the Lock and Home displays, users may opt to install preloaded wallpapers, images, or preferred videos.

1. While on the Home screen, tap and hold the screen before selecting Wallpaper & Style.

2. Select one of the following menus to view the available wallpapers:

- To modify photos, tap the Home screen and Lock screen.

- Wallpaper customization: Choose from an assortment of available wallpapers or download additional ones from the Galaxy Themes.

- Color palette: Determine which hues to use in your wallpapers when selecting a palette.

- If Dark mode has been enabled, dim the wallpaper by activating the function to apply the dark modes to the wallpaper.

Themes

Wallpapers, application icons, and themes to be utilized on the Lock and Home displays can be configured.

1. While on the Home interface, press and hold the screen.

2. Touch a theme after selecting 🔨 Themes to view and download it.

3. To view downloaded themes, select ▦ Menu > My things > Themes from the Screen.

4. Tap a theme, and then tap Apply to have that theme implemented.

Icon

By applying distinct icon sets, the default icons are replaced.

1. Hold the screen down on the Home screen.

2. Touch the icon set after navigating to 🔨 Themes > Icons to view and download it.

3. To view downloaded icons, select ▦ Menu > My Apps > Icons from the menu.

4. Tap an icon, and then press the Apply button to implement the selected icon set.

Widget

Incorporate elements into the home screen to provide expedited access to applications or information.

1. While on the Home interface, press and hold the screen.

2. To activate widget sets, select Touch Widgets and tap the widget sets.

3. Simply swipe to the desired widget and select Add to add it to the Home screen.

Personalized Widgets

It is possible to modify the widget's functionality and placement after it has been added.

o Touch an option while holding down a widget from the Home screen:

- : To generate a stack, supplement the existing elements with identical dimensions and position them precisely at the same location on the screen.

- 🗑 Delete: Eliminate the widget from the display.

- ⚙ Settings: Permits the modification of the elements' appearance and functionality.

- ⓘ App details: Examine the widget's usage, permissions, and more.

Home screen settings

Personalize the Home and Applications displays.

1. While on the Home interface, press and hold the screen.

2. Touch ⚙ Settings to modify the following:

- Configure the home screens: Define separate Home and applications screens for the device, or utilize the Home screen exclusively, which contains all application icons.

- The grid of the Home screen: Select configurations to determine the arrangement of icons on the Home screen.

33

- Grid of the Applications screen: Choose configurations to determine the arrangement of icons on the Applications screen.

- The Folder grid: In order to determine the arrangement of folders, select layouts.

- To display media pages on Home screens, swipe to the right from the Home screen once the feature is enabled. In order to access media services, one must touch.

- Incorporate an Applications screen button into Home screens: Incorporate a button into your Home screens to access our Applications screen easily.

- Locking Home screen layout: Prevents the repositioning or removal of elements from your Home screens.

- Appearance on the Home screen: Automatically append recently downloaded applications to the Home screen.

- In order to conceal applications from the Home and Applications displays, select the desired applications. Return to this screen in order to retrieve concealed applications. Hidden applications continue to be deployed and may appear in Finder search results.

- Activate application icon badges to have badges displayed on applications that have active alerts. Additionally, you can choose badge designs.

- Swipe downward to access the notification pane: To access the notification pane, activate this feature by swiping downward from any location on the home screen.

- Adapting to landscape modes: When the device's orientation is changed from portrait to landscape, the Home screen will rotate automatically.

- Regarding the Home screen, consult the version details.

- Call us: Samsung members can reach Samsung support via telephone.

Simple mode

The layout of Easy mode features larger text and icons, resulting in a more natural visual experience. Change the configuration of your screen from the default to a significantly simpler one.

Recent apps ——————— Back

Home

1. Select Easy mode from the ⚙ Display menu in the preferences menu.

2. To activate this feature, simply touch .
The following alternatives appear:

- Touch & hold delay: Establish the period of time during which consecutive interactions will be recognized as touch & hold events.

- Keyboard with high contrast: Opt for a keyboard featuring colors with high contrast.

Status Bar

This displays device information on the right and alerts for notifications on the left.

Status symbols

Notification icon

Easily configure display options for the Status bar.

Tip: For the configuration of the notifications displayed in the Status bar, navigate to More options > Status bar from the Quick settings menu.

Notification panel

To promptly retrieve information such as settings and notifications, navigate to the Notification panel.

View the notification panel

The Notification pane is accessible from every interface.

1. Swipe the display downward to reveal the Notification pane.

- Touch any item in order to activate it.

- To delete a single notification, drag it to the right or left.

- Tap Clear to dismiss all notifications.

- To modify notifications, select the Notifications settings option.

2. Touch ⟨Back or drag up from the bottom of the display to simply dismiss the Notification panel.

Quick settings

The Notification Pane, which makes use of Quick settings, offers quick access to the device's functions. The icons that follow represent the most frequently used settings accessible via Quick settings. The colors of the icons alter as they are deactivated and activated. There may be additional settings accessible on your device.

1. By dragging the Status bar downward, the Notification pane will appear.

2. Again, swiping downward from the top of the screen will reveal the Quick settings.

- To activate or deactivate the fast settings icon, simply tap it.

- To access the fast setting, press and hold its icon.

Quick settings options

The following options can be accessed via Quick preferences.

- Finders: Conduct a device search.

- Power-off: Options to restart and power off.

- Settings: Navigate to the device's settings menu with ease.

- Additional choices: rearrange quick settings and modify button layout.

- The Device control: Oversee the operation of additional devices that have been equipped with compatible applications, such as Google Home or SmartThings.

- Media outputs: Manage the playback of connected audio and video devices and access the Media pane.

41

- Lightness sliders: Adjust the screen's luminance by dragging.

Bixby

This is a user-adaptive online assistant that develops, learns, and evolves. It identifies your routines, facilitates the setting of location- and time-based reminders, and is integrated into your preferred applications.

- ○ While on the Home interface, utilize the Side key.

Bixby vision

This Bixby is integrated with the user's Internet applications, Gallery, and camera to provide a more comprehensive view of what is visible. Contextual icons are provided for purchasing, translation, QR code detection, and landmark recognition.

Cameras

The camera features Bixby's Vision, which can be accessed through the viewfinder to assist in the interpretation of visual stimuli.

o Follow the on-screen instructions after selecting More > Bixby Vision from the Camera.

Gallery

Utilize the Bixby Vision with images and photographs stored in the Gallery application.

1. To access an image from the Gallery, simply tap on it.

2. Utilize Bixby Vision and adhere to the on-screen instructions.

Internet

Additionally, Bixby Vision enables you to learn more about an image that you encounter through an online application.

1. Hold down an image downloaded from the Internet until a pop-up menu appears.

2. Touch Search while utilizing Bixby Vision, then adhere to the on-screen instructions.

Routines & Modes

Configure modes and routines to modify the device's settings automatically in response to the current activity or circumstance.

- o In the Settings menu, select ✅Modes & Routines for the following pages:

- Modes: Choose a mode in accordance with your current activity or location.

- Routines: One can establish smartphone routines based on specific locations or times.

Digital Wellbeing and Parental Controls

One can easily oversee and regulate digital practices by accessing daily reports that detail the frequency of application usage, the quantity of notifications received, and the frequency of device checks. Additionally, you can program your device to aid in your relaxation even prior to retiring to bed.

○ Tap ⊙ Digital Wellbeing & Parental Control in the Settings menu to access the following features:

- To view the Dashboard, select Dashboard.
  - Screen time: Observe the duration of application launch and daily usage.
  - Notifications received: Peruse the daily count of notifications delivered by applications.
  - Count of Launches or Unlocks: View the daily count of launches of the application.
- The Screens time goal: Establish a time goal for the screens and observe your daily average.
- Application timers: Establish a daily restriction on the amount of time spent on each application.
- Driving monitor: Identify frequently used applications and monitor screen time while connected to the Bluetooth of your vehicle.
- Volume monitor: To protect your ears and keep account of the volume, select the sound source.

- Parental controls: Utilize Google's Families Link application to oversee your child's digital activities. It was possible to select applications, configure content filters, monitor screen time, and limit screen duration.

Always On Display

By utilizing Always-On-Display (AOD), one can access missed call and message notifications, verify the time and date, and view additional customized information without the need to activate the device.

1. Tap 🔒 Lock screen > then Always-On-Display in the Settings menu.

2. Touch ⬤ to activate the feature, and then configure the following settings:

- Determine whether a timer and notifications should be displayed when the device is not in use.

- Clock design: Modify the color and style options for the lock screen and always-on-display clock.

- Present music information: Present music information while the audio controllers of FaceWidgets are in active operation.

- Screen orientation: Present AOD in portrait or landscape format.

- Automatic brightness: Modify the Always-On-Display's luminance automatically.

- Concerning Always-On-Display: Obtain the current software version and license details.

AOD theme

use a personalized theme for the Always-On-Display.

1. Hold the Home screen down and select 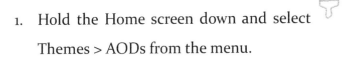 Themes > AODs from the menu.

- To preview and download an AOD into My Always-On-Displays, simply touch the AOD.

2. In order to view downloaded themes, select Menu > My things > AODs.

3. After touching an AOD, select Apply.

Chapter Two

Biometric security

Make use of biometrics to sign in to accounts and unlock devices securely.

Face recognition

The screen can be unlocked by enabling this option. In order to activate the device using your face, you must configure a PIN, pattern, or password.

- Facial recognition technology lacks the security of passwords, PINs, and patterns. Your electronic device might be activated by an entity or individual bearing a striking resemblance to you.

- Face recognition may be impaired by conditions such as the use of heavy makeup, hats, spectacles, or beards.

- When registering faces, ensure that you are in a well-lit area and that the camera lens is squeaky clean.

1. Tap ⬭ Security & privacy in the Settings menu, then select Biometrics, followed by Face recognition.

2. Comply with the instructions to enable face registration.

Face recognition management

Personalize the operation of face recognition.

o In the Settings menu, navigate to ⬭ Security & Privacy > Biometrics > Face recognition.

• Eliminate face data by removing current faces.

• Introduce a distinct appearance to improve recognition: Introduce a distinct appearance to improve facial recognition.

• Face unlock: Enable or disable the security of facial recognition.

• Remain in the lock screen until swiping: If face recognition is used to unlock the device, remain in the lock screen until swiping the screen.

• Visage recognition would only be able to identify your visage if you had your eyes open.

- Enhance screen brightness: Temporarily augment the screen's luminosity to ensure face detection in low-light conditions.

- Concerning facial recognition: Acquire further knowledge regarding the safeguarding of your device through the utilization of face recognition technology.

Fingerprint scanner

Implement fingerprint recognition in certain applications as an alternative method for entering credentials via keyboard.

Additional security measures include the ability to use your biometrics to verify your identity when logging into your Samsung account. To utilize biometrics for device unlocking, a PIN, password, or pattern must be established.

1. Touch Security & privacy in the Settings menu, then select Biometrics, followed by Fingerprints.

2. Comply with the instructions provided to register your fingerprint.

Fingerprint management

The act of renaming, adding, and removing fingerprints.

- o In the Settings menu, select Security & Privacy > Biometrics > Fingerprints to access the following options:

- The entries for registered fingerprints are located at the top of the list. To rename or delete a fingerprint, one may do so by tapping it.

- To add fingerprints, simply adhere to the provided instructions to register an additional fingerprint.

- Scan the fingerprint that was added to determine if it has been registered.

Fingerprint verification settings

Use fingerprint recognition technology to authenticate users across compatible applications and actions.

- o In the Settings menu, navigate to Security & Privacy > Biometrics > Fingerprints.

- Fingerprint unlock: Unlock your device using your biometrics as identification.

- Fingerprint detection is continuous: Fingerprints can be captured even when the display is inactive.

- Icon display during screen off-state: Exhibit your fingerprint icon during screen off-state.

- Incorporate animations during the activation process: Incorporate an animation during the utilization of fingerprint verification.

- Regarding biometrics: Acquire further knowledge regarding the utilization of fingerprints for device security.

Biometric settings

Configure the preferences pertaining to biometric security options.

○ In the Settings menu, select ⬤ Security & Privacy > Biometrics for the following:

- Effect of unlock transitions: Incorporate transition effects into the user interface when biometrics are used to merely unlock the device.

- Concerning unlocking via biometrics: Acquire further knowledge regarding the safeguarding of your device via biometric means.

Multiple windows

By utilizing multiple applications simultaneously, one can multitask. On the divided screen, applications that support the Multi window feature could be displayed concurrently. You can toggle between your applications and modify the extent of their windows.

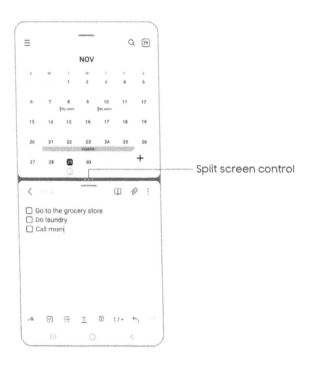

Split screen control

1. From the display, select Recent applications.

2. Tap the application icon, followed by the Open button in split-screen mode.

3. To add an application to split-screen view, tap the application within the other windows.

- To adjust the dimensions of the window, drag the center of its border.

Window control

These window settings modify the appearance of application windows when using a split-screen mode.

1. To resize a window, simply drag the focal point of its border.

2. Touch the window's border's center to access the following options:

- ↑↓ Window swap: Replace the two windows.

- In order to proceed, create and incorporate an application pair shortcut into the Applications edge panel or Home displays.

Edge panel

These include a multitude of customizable compartments that are easily accessible from the screen's edge. In addition to accessing duties, applications, and contacts, the Edge panels also provide access to sports, news, and other information.

- ○ Touch 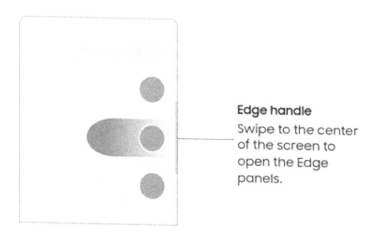 Display > Edge panels from the Settings menu to enable this function.

Edge handle
Swipe to the center of the screen to open the Edge panels.

Apps panel

Applications can be added through the Applications pane.

1. While viewing a screen, pull the Edge handle in the direction of the screen's center. Swipe in order to reveal the Applications pane.

2. To initiate the execution of an application or application pair shortcut, simply touch it. Additionally, you may tap ⋮⋮ All applications to view the complete list of applications.

- To open additional windows in pop-up views, navigate to the open screen and drag the application icon from the Applications pane.

Configure the application window:

1. While viewing a screen, pull the Edge handle toward the screen's center. Swipe in order to reveal the Applications pane.

2. To add additional applications to the Applications pane, select ✎ Edit.

- To add an application to the Applications pane, locate it on the screen's left-hand side and tap it to move it to a location accessible from the right column.

- To create a folder shortcut, drag the application from the left-hand corner of the screen to the upper right-hand column of the application.

- To rearrange the applications in the pane, simply drag each application to its new location.

- To delete an application, select Remove.

3. Tap ‹ Back to save modifications.

Setting up Edge panels

Panels at the edge are customizable.

1. Tap ✿ Display from the Settings menu, then select Edge panels, followed by Panels.

2. The following alternatives are accessible:

- ✔ : Using the checkbox, each pane can be enabled or disabled.

- Set up distinct panels for editing, if available.

- $\mathbb{Q}$: Conduct a search to identify panels that are either deployed or readily available for installation.

- $\vdots$ Additional options:

- To rearrange panels, one can do so by simply repositioning them to the right or left.

- Deleting: Eliminate any downloaded Edge panes from the device.

- Conceal on Lock screens: If a safe screen lock has been established, select panels to conceal on the Lock screen.

- One can easily locate and download supplementary Edge panels from the Galaxy Store.

3. Tap $\langle$ Back to save modifications.

Edge panel position and style

It is possible to relocate the Edge handle.

o Choose the following settings in the Settings menu: Display > Edge panels > Then Handle

- Edge handles: Modify the placement of the Edge handles along the perimeter of the screen by dragging them.

- Position: To determine which side the Edge screens will appear on, select either the Left or Right position.

- Engage the lock function to secure the handle's position and prevent accidental movement while touching and holding.

- Design: Choose a hue for the edge handles.

- Transparency: Modify the Edge handle's transparency by dragging the slider.

- The Size: Modify the Edge handle's size by dragging the slider.

- To adjust the breadth of the Edge handle, use the width slider.

- Produce a vibration when the handle is touched: Generate a vibration when the edge handle is contacted.

Concerning the Edge panels

Edge panel features' current software version and license information are viewable.

- o In the Settings menu, select 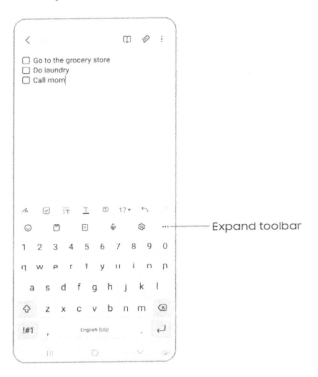 Display > Edge panels > Information regarding the Edge panels.

Enter text

The keyboard or voice can be used to enter content.

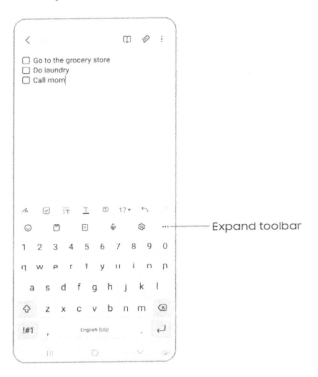

Expand toolbar

The Toolbar

This facilitates rapid access to the keyboard's features. Options are subject to variation among service providers.

- To access the following options, select ••• Expand toolbars from the Samsung keyboard:

- ☺ Expression: Peruse an extensive assortment of GIFs and emoticons, create personalized fusions of emoji, and more.

- ⎙ Clipboard: Provide access to the clipboard.

- ⊡ : For one-handed keyboards, transition to the designated layout.

- 🎤 Voice input: Utilize the voice input capabilities of Samsung.

- ⎚ Split keyboards: Switch to the separated split variant of the keyboard.

- ⎚ Floating keyboards: Modify the keyboard to a floating configuration, allowing for flexible placement across the screen.

- ⚙️ : Access the settings of the keyboard via the settings.

- 🔍 : Search for particular words or phrases within conversations.

- 🔠 Translate: Type words or sentences into the keyboard, and the program will convert them to a different language.

- 🔲 Text extraction: Define and retrieve texts from the selected content.

- Samsung Pass: Enable secure and expedient access to your online account and private information by utilizing biometrics.

- Grammarly: Receive suggestions from Grammarly in real time while you type.

- Emojis: Incorporate an emoji.

- GIF GIFs: Incorporate GIF with animation.

- Bitmoji: Construct a customized emoticon and apply it to the decals.

- : Create your own decals or have those automatically suggested to you by Mojitok.

- Augmented reality emoji: Generate a customized emoji and apply it to the decals.

- Keyboard dimensions: Modify the keyboard's height and breadth.

- Text modification: use an editing pane to assist in identifying specific text that requires duplication, copying, and pasting.

Setting up Samsung keyboards

Configure personalized options for the Samsung keyboard.

- Touch Settings on the Samsung keyboard to access the following options:

- Languages and types: Configure the type of keyboard and select the languages that are visible on the device.

64

- To toggle between languages, merely perform a right or left swipe of the space bar.

Smart typing

- Predictive texts: suggested phrases and words are displayed as you enter.

- One suggestion is to incorporate emoticons when employing predictive text.

- Sticker recommendations during typing: See suggested stickers during typing.

- Automatic replacement: The user's input is automatically substituted with the predictive text recommendations.

- Suggest corrections to the text by underlining misspelled words in red and providing the necessary corrections.

- Text shorthand generation: Produce shortcuts for commonly used phrases.

- Additionally, you can personalize a greater number of typing options.

Arrangement & style

- Toolbars on the keyboard: Display or hide toolbars.

- High contrast keyboards: To increase contrast between the keys and the background, modify the dimensions and color scheme of the Samsung keyboard.

- Themes: Select a keyboard theme.

- Mode: Choose between portrait and landscape orientations.

- Size and transparency: Modify the keyboard's size and transparency.

- Layout: Display special characters and numerals on the keyboard.

- Font sizes can be modified by dragging the slider.

- Custom symbols: Modify keyboard shortcuts for symbols.

Additional options

- Voice input: Establish voice input configurations and services.

- Customize the feedback and touch gestures; swipe and touch.

- Enable the feature that stores captured screenshots in the keyboard's clipboard.

- Select third-party content to utilize: Enable the functionalities of the third-party keyboard.

- Resetting to default configuration: Return the keyboard to its initial state and delete personalized data.

Chapter Three
Camera and Gallery

Capturing Videos and images of superior quality is possible with the Camera application. Images and videos are stored in the Gallery, where they can be viewed and edited.

Camera

Appreciate the complete range of professional lenses and video modes and settings designed for professionals.

○ Select  Camera from the Applications menu.

Tip: Two quick presses of the Side key will initiate the Camera application.

Settings

Zoom

Shooting modes

Gallery

Switch cameras

Capture

Navigate camera screen

Capture breathtaking images with the device's front and rear cameras.

1. Utilize the following controls to configure your shot from the camera:

- Touch the area of the screen where you want the camera to focus.

- Touching the display will reveal the luminance scale. Slider control for adjusting luminance.

- To swiftly toggle between the front and rear cameras, perform a horizontal or vertical motion on the display.

- To adjust the level of zoom, select an option at the bottom of the screen after touching 1x. (Only accessible when the rear camera is engaged.)

- To toggle between photography modes, perform a simple screen swipe to the left or right.

- To modify the settings of your camera, select settings.

2. Navigate to ⭕ Capture.

Setting up the shooting mode

Permits the camera to determine the optimal photography mode or choose from a variety of modes.

- o To modify the shooting mode, swipe the screen to the left and right within 📷 Camera.

- Enjoyable: One can modify their appearance and perspective of the world by utilizing unique Snapchat Lenses.

- The Portrait: For portrait photographs, alter the background.

- Photograph: Permits the camera to determine the optimal photographic settings.

- Video: Permits the camera to determine the optimal video settings.

- Optionally select additional photography modes. To enter and exit shooting modes from the tray located at the bottom of the camera displays, press Add.

– Professional: Manually adjust the exposure value, white balance, ISO sensitivity, and color tone while capturing photographs.

– Macro: Capture images of objects from a distance of three to five centimeters.

– When recording professional videos, manually adjust the ISO sensitivity, white balance, exposure value, and color tone.

– Single take: Capture multiple images and video snippets from different perspectives.

- Panorama: Produce a linear image by accumulating images in a horizontal or vertical orientation.
- Night: Use this to capture images in low-light conditions, obviating the need for a floodlight.
- Food: Capture images that accentuate the vibrant hues of the food.
- Super slow-mo: Captures videos at exceptionally high frame rates to enable high-definition slow-motion playback. It is possible to render a specific segment of a video in slow motion subsequent to its recording.
- Slow motion: Captures videos at exceptionally high frame rates to facilitate slow motion viewing.
- The Hyperlapse: Record at multiple frame rates to produce time-lapse videos. The frame rate can be modified in response to the recorded scene and the device's motion.

AR Zone

Obtain centralized access to every Augmented Reality (AR) feature.

o Navigate to More in ⬤ Camera, and then tap AR Zone. The following capabilities are accessible:

- The AR Emojis Studio: Construct and personalize your My Emojis avatar by utilizing the AR tools.

- The AR Emojis Camera: Generate My Emojis avatars using the camera.

- The AR Emojis Stickers: Enhance My Emojis avatar with the AR stickers.

- AR Doodles are a simple way to enhance videos by incorporating line drawings or handwriting into the environment. AR Doodle observes space and your face to ensure that it is moving in tandem with you.

- The Deco Pic: Real-time enhancement of photographs or videos through the use of the camera.

Record video

Capture lifelike, uninterrupted videos using your device.

1. Swipe left or right within the 📷 Camera to change the filming mode to video.

2. Tap ● Record to initiate video recording.

- To capture an image during a recording session, press 📷 Capture.

- To halt the recording momentarily, press ‖ Pause. To return to the recording session, press ● Resume.

3. Tap Stop when the recording is complete.

Camera settings

To configure the camera's settings, utilize the icons located in the main screen and settings menu.

○ Touch 📷 Camera > Settings to access the following options:

Intelligent functions

- Scene optimizer: Modify the color settings of photographs automatically to correspond with their subjects.

- Shot recommendations: Access on-screen guides that provide guidance on how to align optimal photos.
- QR code scanning: Automatically identify QR codes using the camera.

Photo

- Determine whether to capture burst photos or generate a GIF by swiping the shutter button to the nearest edge.
- The Watermark: Insert a watermark into the photographs' lower left corner.
- High-efficiency images: To conserve space, save images as extremely high-efficiency images. There may be sharing platforms that do not support the format.

Selfies

- Preserve photographs in the same state as when they appear in preview, without the ability to undo them.

Videos

- High-efficiency photographs: To conserve space, save photographs as high-efficiency images. There may be sharing platforms that do not support the format.

- Automatic FPS: Record exceptionally brilliant videos in low-light conditions by simply optimizing the video mode's frame rate automatically.

- Video Stabilization: To maintain focus while the camera is in motion, enable anti-shake.

Generally speaking

- Automatic HDR: Capture supplementary data in the shot's brilliant and dark regions.

- The Grid Lines: Display grid lines in the viewfinder to aid in the composition of a photograph or video.

- One should affix a GPS location tag to their photographs and recordings.

- Shooting methodologies:

- To operate the volume controls, record videos, take photographs, or adjust the volume of the system, press the volume buttons.

- Voice commands: Capture images while uttering important phrases.

- The Floating shutter key: Include an extra shutter button that can be moved to any position on the display.

- Palm display: Extend your hand, palm facing the camera, to promptly capture a photograph within a few seconds.

- Preserve Settings: Determine whether the camera will launch with the same photography modes, angle, filters, and selfie as before.

- The Storage location: Determine where images and videos will be saved.

- Please insert the microSD card (not included) in order to access the storage location.

- Shutter sound: While taking a photograph, play a tone.

- Vibration feedback: Enable vibrations within the Camera application in response to screen touches.

- Enable the Snapchat Lenses in Fun Mode: To incorporate Snapchat lenses and filters into Fun Mode, activate this feature.

Confidentially

- Privacy Notice: Gain access to Samsung's privacy information.

- Permissions: Permissions to access the Camera application are both optional and mandatory.

Others

- Resetting settings: Reset the camera's settings.

- About Camera: Program and hardware information.

- Contact Samsung support by utilizing the Samsung Members phone number.

Gallery

To view all of the visual media stored on your device, navigate to Gallery. Visual and audio files can be edited, viewed, and managed.

- o In the Applications menu, select Gallery.

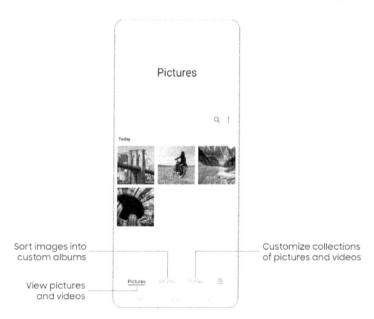

View pictures

Images stored on your device are accessible via the Gallery application.

1. From the Gallery, select Images.

2. Touching an image will reveal it. Swipe left or right to view additional images or videos.

- To activate Bixby Vision in the current image, please touch Bixby Vision.

- To designate an image as a favorite, click the ♡ Add to Favorites button.

- To gain access to the following features, tap More options:

  - View and modify information regarding the photograph.

  - Remaster an image by applying automatic image enhancements to it.

  - Introducing a portrait effect: Utilize the toggle to increase or decrease the visibility of the background in your portrait photographs.

  - Clipboard Copying: Copy an image for pasting into another application.

  - Establish as the background: Designate an image as your background.

  - Proceed by transferring the photographs to secure folders.

- To print a photograph, navigate to a connected printer.

Edit pictures

Enhance your photographs by utilizing Gallery's editing tools.

1. In the ✴ Gallery, select Pictures.

2. To view a photo, tap it, and then tap ✐ Edit to access the following options:

- Utilize automatic adjustments in order to improve the quality of the photograph.

- ⟳ : One may perform various operations such as inverting, rotating, cropping, or more, to alter the overall aspect of the photograph.

- ◌ Filters: Effect coloration.

- ◌ Tone: Modify the exposure, contrast, and luminosity, among others.

- Emojis: Incorporate decals, hand-drawn content, or text.

- Additional choices: Access supplementary editing options.

- Revert: Undo modifications made in order to restore the original image.

3. Tap Save when you have completed the action.

Play video

Access videos stored on the device. Videos can be bookmarked as preferences and video information can be viewed.

1. From the Gallery, select Images.

2. To view a video, merely tap on it. Swipe left or right to view additional images or videos.

- Tap "Add to Favorites" to designate a video as a preference. Following this, the video is added to your Favorites in the Albums tab.

- To gain access to the following features, tap More options:

- Info: View and modify video-related details.

- Play on Video Player: Launch the default video player to view this video.

82

- Wallpaper configuration: Activate a video as the background for your lock screen.

- Proceed by transferring the video to the designated Secure Folder.

3. To initiate the playback of a video, tap ▶ Play video.

Video editing

Videos stored on your device can be edited.

1. Within the ✱ Gallery, select Pictures.

2. To access a video, press the video button.

3. Press ✎ Edit to access the following tools:

- ◁)) Audio: Modify the decibel levels and incorporate ambient music into your videos.

- ▶ : Play to observe a preview of your edited videos.

- Trimming: Remove unwanted segments from the video.

- ⬚ : One may perform various functionalities such as flipping, cropping, rotating, or other

83

alterations to the overall aesthetic of the videos.

- ⊙Filters: Enhance the videos with visual effects.

- Tone: Modify contrast, luminance, exposure, and additional elements.

- Emojis: Incorporate decals, hand-drawn content, or text.

- ⋮:View an expanded array of editing options.

- Revert: Undo any modifications made in order to restore the video to its original state.

4. After clicking "Save," approve if prompted.

Share videos and photos

Images and videos can be shared via the Gallery application.

1. Within the ❋ Gallery, select Pictures.

2. Tap ⋮ More options followed by Edit, then select the images or videos you wish to share.

3. Tap Share, followed by the selection of an application or connection to be used for the sharing selection. Observe the prompts.

Deleting images and videos

Eliminate images and videos from your device.

1. Select Edit from the ⋮ More options menu in ✱ Gallery.

2. To select images and videos, press on them.

3. Tap 🗑 Delete and, if prompted, confirm.

Group similar images together

You can easily organize videos and images in your Gallery according to their similarity.

1. Within the ✱ Gallery, select Group similar images.

2. Press Ungroup similar images to return to the Gallery's view by default.

Screenshot

Take a photograph of the display that you are utilizing. Automatically, the device will produce the Screenshots album within the Gallery application.

o Tap and release the Side and Volume down controls on any display.

Palm slide screenshot

Simply maintain contact with the screen while dragging the corner of your hand from side to side to capture an image of it.

1. To capture, navigate to Advanced features > Motions & gestures > Palm swipe from the Settings menu.

2. Press the button to enable this feature.

Screenshot settings

Modify the settings for screenshots.

o Touch Advanced features in the Settings menu, then select Screenshots & screen recorder.

• Implement a toolbar post-capture: Present additional options subsequent to the capture of a screenshot.

• Erase subsequent to sharing in toolbar: Immediately erase screenshots that have been shared through screenshot toolbars.

- Hide status bars and navigation bars: Prevent the visibility of status bars and navigation bars on the screenshots.

- Preserve the original screenshot: After editing screenshots in the Gallery application, revert to the originals.

- In the format field, select whether the screenshots should be saved in PNG or JPG format.

- Save the screenshots to: Choose the location for screenshot storage.

Screen recorder

Document the activities on your device, make notes, and use your camera to record a video with a self-overlay for sharing with family and friends.

1. Utilize the Quick Settings menu and select Screen recorder.

2. After selecting the desired sound setting, press the Start recording button.

3. The three-second countdown is viable prior to the recording commencing. Pressing the Skip

countdown button would initiate the recording process immediately.

- To create an on-screen drawing, press Draw.

- Select Selfie videos to include any front-facing camera recording.

4. Tap Stop to terminate the recording. These are automatically stored to the Gallery album titled Screens recordings.

Screen recorder settings

Manage the sound and quality settings for the screen recorder.

- o Tap Advanced features in the Settings menu, then select Screenshots & screen recorder.

- The Sound: Using the screen recorder, determine which noises to record.

- Regarding video quality, select a resolution. Choosing a higher quality with a higher resolution will necessitate additional storage space.

- Adjust the slider to easily determine the scale of the video overlay for the selfie.

- Enable this option to indicate screen taps and gestures during a recording.

- Select the storage location where screen recordings will be kept.

Chapter Four
Application

Each application, both preloaded and downloaded, is displayed in the Applications list. Applications could be conveniently downloaded from the Google Play™ and Galaxy Store stores.

o Swiping up from the Home screen will bring you to the Applications list.

Disable or uninstall an application

Applications that are installed can be removed from a device. Specific preloaded applications, which are inherently accessible on the device, can solely be deactivated. Applications that are disabled are deactivated and removed from the Applications list.

o Select an application from the Applications menu, and then tap Uninstall/Disable.

Search application

If you are uncertain of the location of a particular setting or application, you may use the Search function.

1. In the Applications menu, select Search and enter the desired term. As you input, the

screen displays results for compatible settings and applications.

2. Tap a result to access its corresponding application.

Tip: A suggestion for customizing search settings is to navigate to More options > Settings.

Arrange the application

Shortcuts for applications can be arranged in either an alphabetical or a user-specified fashion.

- Within Applications, select More options > Sort to access the following sorting options:
- For custom orders, applications are manually organized.
- Alphabetical order is utilized to sort applications.

Tip: Empty icon spaces can be eliminated from manually ordered (custom order) applications by selecting More options > Clean up the pages.

Create and use folders

In order to organize application alternatives in the Applications list, you could create folders.

1. Hold down an application shortcut in Applications, and then slide it over a different application shortcut until it becomes highlighted.

2. Disable the application shortcut that causes the folder to be created.

- Name of folders: Folders should be named.

- Palette: Modify the color of the folder.

- 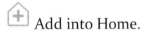Application addition: Insert additional applications into the folder. Select apps by pressing them, and then press Done.

3. In order to exit the folder, press ‹ Back.

Copy folder to any home screen

It is possible to transfer any folder to the Home interface.

o While holding down a folder in Apps, select ⊕ Add into Home.

Delete any folder

Deleted folders restore application shortcuts to the Applications display.

1. Remove a folder by holding down the folder in Applications.

2. Press 🗑 Delete folder and, if prompted, confirm.

Games Booster

Obtain outstanding performance while playing games, contingent on usage. Disable notifications and enable features that improve the overall gaming experience.

Swipe upward from the bottom of the screen while playing a game to access the navigation menu. The following options are displayed on the extreme left and right:

- Touch protections: To prevent inadvertent presses, lock your screen. This option is the default one.

- Game Booster: Configure additional features, including blocking navigation bars, screenshots, and screen interactions, in addition to performance monitoring.

Application settings

Administration of downloaded and preloaded applications.

- ○ In the Settings menu, select ⊞ Apps. Select the following options to personalize:

- • Define default applications: Determine which applications are utilized for various purposes such as messaging, calling, and accessing websites.

- • Samsung application settings: Customize the settings of Samsung applications by viewing lists of them.

- • Applications: Tap an application to view and modify information regarding its privacy and usage preferences. Applications may have distinct options.

Tip: To reset modified application options, select ⋮ More options followed by Reset application preferences.

Calendar

By linking the Calendar app to your multiple online accounts, you can consolidate all of your calendars in a single location.

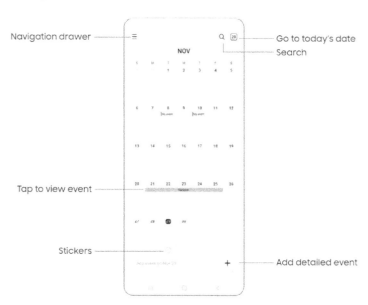

Navigation drawer

Go to today's date

Search

Tap to view event

Stickers

Add detailed event

Add calendar

Accounts can be added to the Calendar application.

1. Touch the Navigation drawer in Calendar.

2. In the Manage calendars menu, select Add account, followed by the desired account type.

3. Enter your account information and proceed with the on-screen instructions.

Note: Accounts may also provide support for email and contacts, among other functionalities.

Calendar notification style

Personalized alerts from the Calendar application are customizable.

1. Select Alert style from the ≡ Navigation drawer of the Calendar by tapping ⚙ Calendar settings.

   The following options can be accessed:

- Light: Receive an alert and briefly hear a sound.
- Medium: Appear on the entire screen and hear a fleeting sound.
- Strong: Appear in full-screen and experience a persistent ring sound until it is deactivated.

2. Depending on the alert design selected previously, the following sound options are available:

- Short sound: For Medium or Light alert styles, select the notifications sound.

- Long Sound: To enable the Strong alerts style, select the alerts sound.

Create an event

Make use of your calendar to establish events.

1. To include an event in the Calendar, select Add comprehensive events from the menu.

2. Enter your event's information, and then click Save.

Delete event

Events may be removed from the Calendar.

1. To modify an event from the Calendar, press and then contact it again.

2. Select Delete and provide confirmation when prompted.

Contact

Maintain and organize contacts. Syncing with private accounts that are added to the device is possible. In addition to supporting calendars and communications, accounts may also provide support for additional functionalities.

Add profile picture

Add, delete, and expand fields

Create a contact

1. Select ╋ Create contact from the  Contacts menu.

2. Enter your contact's information, and then click Save.

Change contact information

You could alter a contact by selecting a field and modifying or deleting information, or by adding additional fields to the contact's information lists.

1. Select a contact from the Contacts menu.

2. Select ✎ Edit.

3. Touch any field to modify, add, or remove data.

4. Select Save.

Favorites

When you designate contacts as favorites, they are consolidated at the highest level of the contact lists and can be easily accessed from any other application.

1. Tap a contact from the Contacts menu.

2. To mark an individual as a preference, press
   ☆ Favorites.

- To eliminate a contact from Favorites, select
  ☆ Favorites.

Share contact details

It is straightforward to share contacts with others through the use of various sharing services and methods.

1. Tap a contact from the 👤 Contacts menu.

2. Select ⟨ Share.

3. Text or vCard files (VCF) should be touched.

4. Select the sharing method and adhere to the instructions provided.

Tip: Tap ⋮ More followed by the QR code while viewing a contact to swiftly forward the information to family and friends. The QR code is automatically updated whenever the contact information fields are modified.

Contacts appear when sharing content

Content can be shared with contacts directly from within any application. When enabled, your standard contacts are displayed in the Share interface.

o To enable the option, navigate to Settings >
Advanced features > Show contacts while
sharing content and tap .

Groups

It is possible to organize contacts using groups.

Form a group

Create groups for intimate contacts.

1. Select Groups from the Show navigation
   menus menu in the Contacts section.

2. Tap Create group, then tap fields to enter group
   information:

- Group name: Provide a name that represents
  your new group.

- Group ringtone: Modify group-specific
  sounds.

- Adding members: Select the contacts that you
  wish to include in the new group, and then
  click Done.

3. Select Save.

Delete or add contacts to a group

It is possible to delete contacts from the group or add new ones.

- o Select a group by selecting Show navigation menus > Groups from the 👤 Contacts menu.

- • To delete a contact, select it by holding down the 🗑 Remove button.

- • To add contacts, select ✏ Edit > Add the member, followed by the desired contacts by touching them. When complete, click Done followed by Save.

Send message to group

It is feasible to transmit text messages to the group members.

1. Touch a group after selecting Show navigation menus > Groups from the 👤 Contacts menu.

2. Select ⋮ More options, followed by Send message.

Send email to group

Communication via email is possible with the group members.

1. Touch a group after selecting ⸺ Show navigation menus > Groups from the 👤 Contacts menu.

2. Select More options followed by Send email.

3. To select contacts, touch them; to select all, tap the All checkbox in the upper-right corner of the screen; then press Done.

   - The display is limited to group members whose records contain email addresses associated with those records.

4. After selecting your email account, proceed with the on-screen instructions.

Deleting a group

A user-created group may be removed.

1. Select ⸺ Show navigation menus > Groups from the 👤 Contacts menu, and then tap a group.

2. Select ⋮ Additional options, and then delete the group.

- To delete a group exclusively, select Delete only group.

- To remove a group and its contacts, select Delete group and transfer the group members to the garbage.

Merge contacts

Integrate contact information from multiple sources into a single contact by linking entries to that contact.

1. Select Manage contacts from the ≡ Show navigation menus menu in the 👤 Contacts menu.

2. Select the Merge contacts button. Duplicate phone numbers, email addresses, and names of the contacts would be grouped together for recording purposes.

3. Select contacts by pressing them, and then tap Merge.

Import contacts

Your contacts can be imported to the device in the form of a vCard file (VCF).

1. Select Manage contacts from the Show navigation menus menu in 👤 Contacts.

2. Select Import contacts and adhere to the on-screen instructions.

Export contacts

Your contacts can be exported from the device in the form of a vCard file (VCF).

1. Select Manage contacts from the ▬ Show navigation menus menu in 👤 Contacts.

2. Navigate to the Export contacts and confirm.

Transferring contacts

It is possible to transfer contacts between your device and SIM card.

1. Select Manage contacts from the ▬ Show navigation menus menu in 👤 Contacts.

2. Select Transfer contacts.

105

3. Tap a position for From & To in order to relocate previously saved contacts.

Contact synchronization

Ensure that all of your contact information is current across all of your accounts.

1. Select Manage contacts from the ☰ Show navigation menus menu in 👤 Contacts.

2. Navigate to Synchronize contacts.

Delete contacts

You may delete a single contact or multiple contacts.

1. To select a contact from the Contacts, keep it down.

- It is also possible to select other contacts for removal by touching them.

2. Select 🗑 Delete and provide confirmation when prompted.

Emergency contacts

It is possible to contact the emergency contacts despite the device being closed.

- Navigate to Safety & emergency > Emergency contacts in the Settings menu.

- Adding a member: Designate the contacts stored in your mobile device as emergency contacts.

- Presentation on Lock screens: Present the emergency contacts in the Lock screen for easy access in the event of an unforeseen circumstance.

Internet

Samsung's Internet is a dependable, quick, and user-friendly web browser for your device. Utilize the browsing capabilities of extremely secure websites, which safeguard your privacy, expedite your searches, and enhance your browsing experience.

Browser tab

Utilize tabs to concurrently access multiple websites.

- ○ From the ● Internet, navigate to 1 Tabs > New tab.

- To close a specific tab, navigate to ⌷① Tabs > ⊗ Close tab.

Make a Bookmark

You can bookmark the websites of your favorites for quick access.

- When using the ◯ Internet, navigate to the page you wish to bookmark and select the ☆ "Add to bookmarks" option.

Open bookmark

Launch web pages quickly from the Bookmarks page.

1. While browsing the web, select ☆ Bookmarks.

2. Navigate to the bookmark.

Save a page

There are multiple alternatives for storing a webpage within the Samsung Internet application.

- From the ◯ Internet, select ☰ Tools > "Add-page-to" to access the following options:

- Incorporate web pages into the Bookmarks directory.

- Quick access: Retrieve inventories of webpages that are frequently accessed or saved.

- Create a shortcut to a specific webpage from the Home interface.

- Stored pages: Ensure that you can access webpage content offline by saving it to your device.

View history

To access lists of recently visited websites:

- o   In the Internet browser, navigate to ≡ Tools > History.

Tip: To delete your browsing histories, select ⋮ More options followed by Clear history.

Share page

Web pages can be shared with contacts.

- o   From the ◯ Internet, select ≡ Tools > Share and proceed with the on-screen instructions.

Secret mode

When you access a page in secret mode, it does not appear in your browser or search history, and it does not leave any traces on your device (such as cookies). The secret tab's displays are rendered in a darker hue than those of the standard tab.

Any downloaded files that persist on your device after the hidden tabs have been closed.

1. From the ⬤ Internet, select ⬜1 Tabs > Secret mode.

2. Selecting the Start button will initiate perusing in Secret mode.

Secret mode settings

To access Secret mode, a biometric safeguard or password is required.

1. While browsing the web, select ⬜1 Tabs.

2. To access the following secret mode settings, select ⋮ More options followed by Secret modes:

- Using password protection: Establish a password to activate secret mode and utilize biometrics.

- To reset Secret mode, remove all Secret mode data and revert to the default settings.

Turn off secret mode

Deactivate the Secret mode and resume your typical browsing experience.

o While browsing the ⬤ Internet, select 1️⃣ Tabs > Secret mode, and then exit.

Internet settings

Modify the configurations associated with the Internet application's use.

o To access the Settings menu from the ⬤ Internet, select ≡ Tools > Settings.

Message

Communicate with contacts effortlessly through the Messages application by sharing photos, sending emojis, or simply exchanging brief greetings. Options are subject to variation among service providers.

- o Select Compose new messages from the  Messages menu.

Search messages

To efficiently locate a message, utilize the search function.

1. Within Messages, navigate to Search.

2. After entering keywords into the Search field, press the Search key on your keyboard.

Delete conversation

In order to eliminate conversion histories, delete the conversations.

1. Select Delete from the ⋮ More options menu in the 💬 Messages section.

2. To delete a conversation, tap each one.

3. Select 🗑 Delete all and provide confirmation when prompted.

Emergency message

It is possible to transmit visual and auditory communications to emergency contacts.

o In the Settings menu, select 🔔 Safety & Emergency > Emergency SOS. Enable the following by tapping the button five times:

• The Countdown: Select durations in seconds before activating critical operations.

• When making urgent phone calls: Select contact numbers for any urgent inquiries.

- To disseminate information to emergency contacts, activate the feature that transmits location data to said contacts.

Tip: Additionally, the Emergency SOS can be activated by simultaneously tapping the Volume and Side buttons down and then selecting Emergency call.

Message settings

Configure multimedia and text message settings.

o Select Settings from the ⋮ More options menu in the 💬 Messages.

Emergency alert

These provide warning of impending dangers and other situations. No fees are associated with the receipt of emergency notifications.

o To modify emergency alert notifications, navigate to ⚠ Safety & emergency > Wireless-Emergency-Alerts from the Settings menu.

Tip: It is also possible to access emergency alerts through the Notifications menu. Select 💬

Notifications > Advanced settings > Wireless-Emergency-Alerts from the Settings menu.

My File

Manage and access the files, including photos, videos, music, and audio files, that are stored on your device. Additionally, files stored in cloud accounts are accessible and manageable.

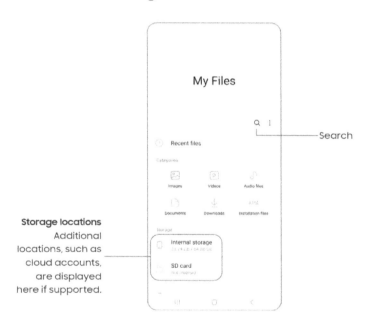

File group

The files that are present on your device are categorized as follows:

- Recently accessed files: View the files that were accessed recently.

  – This selection is displayed in the event that a minimum of one file has been accessed in the recent past.

- View files in categories based on their file type.

- The Storage: Access the files stored in the cloud accounts and, optionally, an SD card of your device.

  – Cloud accounts may differ depending on the services to which you gain access.

- Trash: Make the decision regarding whether to recover or delete deleted files permanently.

- Storage analysis entails determining what is occupying space on the storage.

My Files settings

Apply this to modify file administration settings, among others. Options are contingent upon the service provider.

o From the ⬜ My Files menu, select More options followed by Settings for the following options:

- Accounts in the cloud: Connect to and manage cloud services.

- File administration: Tailor the deletion, display, and access of files to the mobile data.

- In the process of analyzing storage, select the file size that you wish to flag.

- Privacy: My Files access permissions.

Telephone

An application for a smartphone does considerably more than facilitate phone calls. You may investigate options for advanced calling.

Calls

A smartphone application that allows you to make and receive calls from the Contacts tab, Home screen, and Recents, among other locations.

Make a call

One can utilize their smartphone to initiate and receive calls directly from the Home screen.

- o In the 📞 Phone menu, enter a number using the keypad and then tap 📞 Call.
- • If the keypad is not visible, press Touch Keypad.

Make a call from recent calls

All incoming, outgoing, and missed calls are documented in the Call log.

1. Select Recents from the Phone menu to view lists of recent calls.

2. After touching the contact, press the 📞 Call button.

Make a call from your contacts

You can initiate a phone call to a contact directly through the Contacts application.

- o To initiate a call from a contact, simply swipe the finger to the right of the contact in the 👤 Contacts menu.

Answer a call

The smartphone rings and displays the name or phone number of the caller whenever it receives a call. In the context of application usage, the pop-up screen is presented to indicate an incoming call.

o   To answer an incoming call, scroll the Answer button to the right on the screen.

Tip: To answer an incoming call, press the Answer button on the pop-up screen that appears during the call.

Reject call

You are free to decline any incoming telephone call. The incoming call is displayed in a pop-up screen while the application is in use.

o   Sliding the Decline button to the left on the incoming call screen will cause the call to be rejected and routed to voicemail.

Tip: Press Decline on incoming pop-up screens to reject calls and have them routed to voicemail.

Reject a call and leave a message

It is possible to decline incoming calls via text message response.

- o While on the screen for an incoming call, select Send message by sliding it to the top.

Tip: On the pop-up screen of an incoming call, select Send message and then enter a message.

End call

- o Click the 😔 "End call" button when you are prepared to terminate the call.

Actions while on a call

Aside from multitasking, you could adjust the call's volume, switch to a headset or speaker, and adjust the call's volume.

- o To adjust the volume level, press and hold the Volume buttons.

Switch to speaker or headphones

Utilize a Bluetooth headset or speaker to receive your calls (this is not included).

- o To listen to a caller through the speaker, select 🔊 the Speaker option. Alternatively, to utilize Bluetooth headsets, select the Bluetooth option.

Perform multiple tasks

When you exit the call screen to access another application, the Status bar will still display your active calls.

In order to return to the phone call screen:

o Slide the Status bar downward to bring up the Notification Pane, then tap the call to initiate it.

For terminating a multitasking call:

o To bring up the Notification pane, drag the Status bar downward, and then press End call.

Call background

Choose an image or video to display whenever you make or receive a phone call.

o From the Phone app, select More options > Settings > Calls background to access the following options:

- Layout: Determine how caller information should be presented in the case where the individual has a profile photograph.

- Background: Select an image to be presented during a teleconference.

Call pop-up settings

Calls that are being received concurrently with the use of other applications may manifest as pop-up windows.

- ○ Press More options on the phone, then tap Settings, followed by Call display when using applications. The following options can be accessed:

- Full screen: Displays incoming calls in the Phone application's full screen.

- Small pop-up: Display incoming calls in the upper-right corner of the display as a pop-up.

- Display incoming calls in the form of miniature pop-ups.

- Maintaining calls in pop-up: Enable this setting to retain phone calls in your pop-up even after they have been answered.

Manage calls

Your phone calls are being recorded in the call log. It is possible to set up speed dials, use voicemail, and block calls.

Call records

In your Call log, the number of phone calls that you have made, missed, or received is recorded.

o In the Phone menu, select Recents. A list of the most recent phone calls you have made appears. When a caller is present on your Contacts list, their name is displayed.

Save contacts information from last call

Utilize recent phone call information to establish communication or to update the Contacts list.

1. Under Phone, select Recents.
2. Select the phone call whose details you wish to include in your Contacts' lists, and then click "Add to contacts."

3. Select Update an existing contact or Create a new contact.

Delete call recording

For removing entries from call logs:

1. In the Phone's menu, select Recents.

2. Retain the call in question in order to delete it from your Call log.

3. Hit the Delete button.

Block number

When a caller is added to a block list, any subsequent calls from that number are routed directly to voicemail, and any messages they send are not received.

1. On the mobile device, select Recents.

2. To add a caller to the Block list, touch that individual and then tap Details.

3. Select Block, followed by More > Block contact, and confirm when prompted.

Note: It is also possible to modify your Block lists from the Settings menu. From the mobile device, select More options > Settings > Block numbers.

Speed dial

Contacts could be designated shortcut numbers to facilitate speed dialing of their default numbers.

1. Touch the Keypad on the phone, then select More options, followed by the Speed dial number option. The designated speed dial numbers are displayed on the screen of your speed dial number.

2. Make contact with the unassigned number.

- To select an alternate Speed-dial number instead of the following one, press ▼ Menu.

- The first position is designated exclusively for voicemail.

3. Input a name or number, or select Add from the Contacts menu, to associate a contact with that number.

127

- The selected contact is displayed in the "Speed dial numbers" window.

Make a call using speed dial

It is possible to initiate a contact using the Speed dial.

- While on the phone, maintain pressure on the speed dial number.

- Input the first digits of a speed dial number that is at least one digit long, and then holds down the last digit.

Delete speed dial number

The removal of any assigned speed-dial number is possible.

1. Press More options followed by Speed-dial numbers in the Phone menu.

2. Simply press Delete next to the contact whose speed dial entry you wish to remove.

Emergency call

In your area, it is possible to contact an emergency cell phone number regardless of the service status of the device. In the event of phone deactivation, only emergency calls are permitted.

1. Dial the emergency cell phone number into the telephone (9-1-1 in North America) and press the Call button.

2. Remain on the contact. During this type of call, the preponderance of in-call features are accessible.

Note: The emergency cell phone number remains diallable regardless of the cell phone's lock status, allowing unauthorized individuals to utilize your device to request assistance in the event of an emergency. When accessed directly from the locked screen, the receiver would only have access to the emergency calling features. The remainder of the mobile phone is still safeguarded.

Phone settings

These allow you to modify configurations associated with your mobile application.

o   Select Settings from the ⠿ More options menu on the Ⓒ Phone.

Make a multi-party call

Perform additional phone conversations while one is in progress. Options are contingent upon the service provider.

1. To initiate a second conversation, select ╋ Add phone call from the menu of active calls.

2. Enter the new number and press the ☎ Call button. Upon the caller being answered:

-   To switch between two contacts, press the ⟲ Swap or On-hold button.

-   To enable simultaneous audio for both callers, press the ⤳ Merge button (this is multi-conferencing).

Video call

To facilitate video calls:

○ Press the 📞 Phone button, enter a number, and then select 📹 Meet or ⭕ Video calls.

Please note that not all devices are compatible with video conferencing. The recipient may choose to receive the video call or respond to calls using the standard voice mode.

Video call effect

In some available applications, you can modify or obscure your background while a video call is in progress.

1. Select Video call effects from the ⭕ Advanced features menu in the Settings menu.

2. Touch ⬭ to activate this function.

3. Choose a readily available option:

- Background color: The virtual background can be transformed into a solid color automatically in response to the environment.

- Background image: Choose an image from your personal collection to be used as the background for video calls.

Wi-Fi calling

It is possible to conduct phone conversations while connected to a Wi-Fi network.

1. To enable Wi-Fi calling on your phone, select ⋮ More options > Settings > Wi-Fi calling.

2. Touch this feature to activate it.

3. Follow the on-screen instructions to configure and set up Wi-Fi calling.

RTT (Real-Time Text)

Real-time input and response exchange with another individual while on the phone.

RTT functionality is available when making a phone call to an individual whose smartphone supports RTT and is connected to a teletypewriter (TTY) device. The RTT icon is present on all incoming RTT telephone conversations.

1. Select Settings from the More options menu on the Phone.

2. Press Real-time text to access the following options:

- RTT call key: Select the appropriate visibility settings.
- Conspicuous solely during phone calls: exhibit the RTT call key.
- Display the RTT call key at all times, both on the keypad and during calls.
- Use external TTY keyboards: When external TTY keyboards are connected, conceal your RTT keyboard.
- TTY modes: Select the desired TTY modes for the active keyboards.

Samsung Health

Utilize Samsung's Health to strategize and oversee various facets of daily life that promote health, including sleep, physical activity, and nourishment.

Notification: The data collected from the device, Samsung's Health, or related software is not intended for use in disease diagnosis or other medical conditions, nor in the prevention, treatment, mitigation, or cure of diseases.

The accuracy of the information and data provided by this device and its corresponding software may be impacted by environmental conditions, specific actions performed while using or wearing the device, device settings, user configuration or information provided by the user, and various end-user interactions.

Before beginning a workout

While Samsung's Health application serves as a commendable companion to an exercise regimen, it is advisable to consult a physician prior to commencing any physical activity. Although some individuals may find light physical activity, such as moderate walking, to be safe, it is strongly advised that you consult your physician prior to starting an exercise regimen, especially if you have any of the following medical conditions:

- Arthritis; Heart disease; Asthma or any form of respiratory disease; Liver or kidney disease; Diabetes; and Diabetes.

Before beginning an exercise regimen, you should consult your physician if you have any of the following symptoms that indicate a serious illness of the lungs, heart, or other organs:

It is recommended that prior to beginning any exercise regimen, you consult with your physician or medical practitioner. If you are unsure of your health status, are pregnant, or have any other health issues, you must consult your physician before commencing a new exercise regimen.

Notes

Create notes containing text, images with footnotes, vocal recordings, and music using Samsung Notes. Easily disseminate your notes through social networking sites.

Incorporate the following into a note: text, images accompanied by annotations, audio, and visual recordings. Sharing the notes on social networking sites is a simple process.

Create a note

Incorporate text, images, voice recordings, and more.

1. Select ⬚ Add from the ⬛ Samsung Notes menu.

2. Make use of the available text options to generate content.

Voice recording

Produce recordings of annotated voice that are well-suited for use in lectures and meetings. Maintain a journal while recording audio. Synchronized playback directs the user to the corresponding text.

1. To add an item to Samsung Notes, select ⬚ Add.

2. Select ⬚ Insert followed by Voice recording.

3. Leverage the text options at your disposal to generate content while recording an audio file.

Edit notes

Modify the notes that you have generated.

1. To display a note from the ⬛ Samsung Notes, the user must contact the note.

2. Tap ⬚ Edit to make modifications.

137

3. When finished, press the ⟨Navigate upward button.

Note options

It is possible to organize, modify, and oversee the notes.

o Accessible from the Samsung Notes are the following options:

- ⊡⁺: Initiate the import of a PDF file onto Samsung Notes.

- 🔍 Search: Conduct a keyword search.

- ⋮ Additional options:

- Edit: Select the notes that you wish to lock, delete, share, or save as files.

- View: Navigate between simple, grid, and list views.

- Highlight preferred notes: Position the notes that have been annotated as preferences in the uppermost section of your homepage.

Note menu

It is possible to observe notes exclusively by category.

- In the Samsung Notes, select Display navigation menus for the following options:

- Samsung's Notes settings: Gain access to the Samsung Notes application's settings.

- Access the entirety of the notes.

- Shared notebook: Through Samsung's account, access notebooks that have been shared with contacts.

- Trash: Retrieve deleted notes that have been inaccessible for a period of 15 days at most.

- Folders: Easily navigate through the notes by group.

- Folder management consists of adding, removing, and organizing folders.

Access Settings

The settings of your device can be accessed in various methods.

- Swipe downward from the Home screen and select ⚙ Settings.

- In the Applications menu, select ◉ Settings.

Search settings

When uncertain of the precise location of a particular setting, one may conduct a search for it.

1. Tap 🔍 Search in the Settings menu and enter relevant keywords.

2. Tap entry to navigate to the specified setting.

Connection

You have the ability to administer the connections between your device and multiple networks, in addition to other devices.

Wi-Fi

It is possible to connect a device to a Wi-Fi network for Internet access without the need to utilize mobile data.

1. In the Settings menu, navigate to Connections, select Wi-Fi, and then press to enable Wi-Fi and scan for available networks.
2. Touch a network and, when prompted, enter a password.
3. Select Connect.

Connect to a hidden wireless network

You can link to the intended Wi-Fi network even if it is not visible in the scan results by entering its information manually. Request the Wi-Fi network administrator's name and password prior to beginning.

1. In the Settings menu, navigate to Connections, select Wi-Fi, and then press to activate Wi-Fi.

2. Select the ✛ Add network option at the bottom of the list.

3. Enter details regarding Wi-Fi networks:

• Network name: Provide the exact name of the network.

• Security: Select the requisite security options from the menus and enter the corresponding password when prompted.

• Password: Enter the password for the network.

• Covert networks: Establish a covert network.

• Expanding the scope: Establish supplementary advanced configurations, including proxy and IP settings.

4. Select Save.

Tip: To connect to a Wi-Fi network, simply use the camera on your device to scan the QR codes and press ⌖ Scan QR codes.

Intelligent Wi-Fi Setting

One has the ability to establish connections to various types of Wi-Fi networks and hotspots, administer saved networks, and access the network addresses of their device. Options are contingent upon the service provider.

1. To enable Wi-Fi, navigate to 🛜 Connections > Wi-Fi from the Settings menu, and then press ⬤.

2. Select More options, followed by Intelligent Wi-Fi, to access the following options:

- Transitioning to mobile data: Should this feature be activated, your device will utilize mobile data in the event of an unstable Wi-Fi connection. When your Wi-Fi signal is exceptionally robust, it returns to that signal.

- Automated switching to Wi-Fi networks that are significantly quicker or more stable is recommended.

- Automatically Turn Wi-Fi On or Off: Enable Wi-Fi in frequently visited areas.

- Present network quality information: In the inventories of accessible Wi-Fi networks, include network information such as stability and speed.

- Identify dubious networks: Be notified in the event that suspicious activity is identified within the current Wi-Fi network.

- Automatic Hotspot Connection: Establish an automatic connection to a detected Wi-Fi hotspot.

- Intelligent Wi-Fi: Gain access to versions of intelligent Wi-Fi.

Advanced Wireless Settings

It is possible to establish connections to various types of Wi-Fi networks and hotspots, administer networks that have been saved, and locate the network address of a device. Options are contingent upon the service provider.

1. In the Settings menu, navigate to Connections, select Wi-Fi, and then press to enable Wi-Fi.

2. Select Additional options, followed by the Advanced option for the following:

• Synchronize with the Samsung Cloud or account: Utilize your Samsung account to synchronize Wi-Fi profiles.

• Display the Wi-Fi pop-up: Inform the user that Wi-Fi is available prior to application launch.

• Wi-Fi or network notifications: Receive alerts whenever observable open networks within your range.

• Network management: Gain access to saved Wi-Fi networks and configure the option to reconnect automatically or forget about the specific networks.

- The Wi-Fi on/off histories: Examine applications that have recently activated or deactivated your Wi-Fi.

- Automatically establish connections with Wi-Fi networks that are compatible with Hotspot 2.0.

- Authentication certificates must be installed prior to installing network certificates.

Wi-Fi Direct

This enables devices to easily exchange data via Wi-Fi.

1. In the Settings menu, navigate to Connections, select Wi-Fi, and then press to activate Wi-Fi.

2. Select More options, followed by Wi-Fi Direct.

3. Touch a device and then follow the on-screen instructions to establish a connection.

Disconnect Wi-Fi Direct

It is possible to detach your device from the Wi-Fi Direct device.

o Navigate to Connections > Wi-Fi > More options > Wi-Fi Direct from the Settings menu. To detach a device, one must apply pressure to the device.

Bluetooth

One possible pairing option is with another Bluetooth-enabled device, such as Bluetooth headphones or an automobile infotainment system. Once a connection has been established, the devices are able to retrieve and exchange information without the need to re-enter the passkey.

1. Touch Bluetooth in the Connections menu, followed by this button , to enable Bluetooth.

2. To connect, simply touch a device and follow the on-screen instructions.

• To disengage from the paired device, select the Disconnect button. To reconnect, press the Connect button.

Tip: To enable this function when sharing a file, simply tap the Bluetooth button.

Rename paired device

It is possible to rename the associated device in order to greatly simplify its identification.

1. In the Settings menu, navigate to Connections, tap Bluetooth, and then press to enable Bluetooth.

2. Select ⚙ Settings in the vicinity of the device's name, followed by Rename.

3. Rename after entering the new name.

Unpairing a Bluetooth device

When disconnecting from a Bluetooth device, both devices will no longer recognize each other, and you will need to reconnect the connection by pairing the devices together again.

1. To enable Bluetooth, navigate to Connections > Touch Bluetooth from the Settings menu, and then press .

2. Select Settings in close proximity to the device, followed by Unpair.

3. To confirm, merely tap Unpair.

Advanced Bluetooth settings

Additional Bluetooth configurations can be found in the Advanced menus.

1. In the Settings menu, navigate to Connections > Bluetooth.

2. To access the following options, select Advanced settings > ⋮ More options > Advanced settings.

- Synchronize with the Samsung Cloud or account: Sync files with the Samsung account that were transferred via Bluetooth.

- Phone's name: Modify the device's moniker to reflect the Bluetooth connections.

- Retrieve inventories of files that have been acquired via Bluetooth.

- Music Sharing: Permit companions to utilize your Bluetooth device's speaker or headphones to play music.

- Ringtone synchronization: When receiving phone calls via the linked Bluetooth device, utilize the ringtones configured on the device.

- The Bluetooth control histories allow you to view applications that have recently utilized Bluetooth.

- Blocking pairing requests: To restrict pairing requests, you can add gadgets.

- The Bluetooth scan histories provide the ability to manage Bluetooth options for applications and see which applications have recently scanned for nearby Bluetooth devices.

Double audio

You could stream audio from your device to two Bluetooth audio devices that are connected.

1. Connect Bluetooth audio devices to the device.

2. In the Notifications panel, select Media output.

3. In the Audio output, select adjacent to each audio device (approximately two devices) to play audio to them.

Near Field Communication and Payment

NFC (Near Fields Communication) facilitates interaction with other devices even in the absence of a network connection. This technology is specifically employed by Android Beam and specific payment applications. In addition to supporting NFC, the device to which you are sending must be within 4cm of the transmitting device.

○ To enable this feature, navigate to Settings > Connections > Touch NFC in addition to contactless payments, and then press .

Click and pay

Pay with an NFC payment application by simply connecting your device to a credit card reader that is compatible.

Utilize NFC payment software to complete transactions by simply pressing your device against a compatible credit card reader.

1. To enable NFC, navigate to Connections in the Settings menu, select NFC alongside contactless payments, and then press .

2. Touch Contactless payments to display the application that is used by default for payments.

- To utilize an additional payment application, select it by tapping one that is already present.

- To utilize a newly launched payment application, tap Pay while the application is in the process of opening.

- To designate a different payment service as the default, select Others and then the desired service.

Airplane mode

This deactivates all network connections, including Bluetooth, Wi-Fi, mobile data, and messaging and calling. After Airplane mode has been enabled, Wi-Fi and Bluetooth can be enabled via the Quick settings pane or the Settings menu.

- o In the Settings menu, navigate to Connections, select Airplane mode, and then press to activate this function.

Note: Mobile device usage while traveling by air or sea may be governed by applicable local and federal regulations and restrictions. In airplane mode, all network connectivity would be deactivated. Ultra-wideband frequencies are not permitted on aircraft or ships and can be deactivated using the Airplane mode. Always consult the appropriate authorities and adhere to the crew's directives regarding when and how to utilize the device.

Mobile network

Leverage mobile networks to configure your device to establish a connection with them and utilize mobile data. Options are contingent upon the service provider.

- o Select Mobile networks from the 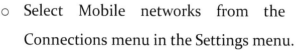 Connections menu in the Settings menu.
- Mobile data: Enable the use of mobile data.
- Voice, text, and data roam configurations must be modified to accommodate international roaming.
- Data roaming: Make a decision regarding whether to allow your device to connect to mobile data while you are outside the service provider's network area.
- Roaming data access: Configure mobile network access while roaming.
- Network modes: The mobile device has the ability to select which network mode to utilize.
- Access Point Names (APNs): Choose or include the APNs that contain the necessary

network configurations for your device to establish a connection with the server.

- Network operators: Determine which networks are available and which are preferred.

- For troubleshooting purposes, gather usage and diagnostic data pertaining to mobile networks.

- A network extender merely performs a scan for cells capable of extending the network connection.

Tip: Employ these functionalities to assist you in overseeing the connection configurations that could potentially affect your monthly invoices.

Mobile hotspot

This process utilizes the data plans in order to establish a Wi-Fi network that is accessible to numerous devices.

1. In the Settings menu, select 📶 Connections, and then Mobile hotspot & tethering, followed by Mobile hotspot.

2. To activate a mobile hotspot, press ⬤▬.

3. On the devices to which you wish to connect, activate Wi-Fi and select the mobile hotspot for your device. Connect by entering the password for the mobile hotspot.

- A inventory of connected devices can be found under the heading Connected devices.

Tip: To connect an additional device to the mobile hotspot, merely scan the ▦ QR code rather than entering the password.

Configure mobile hotspot settings

The mobile hotspot's connection and security configurations could be modified.

1. Select Mobile hotspot & tethering from the
   ![icon] Connections menu, followed by Mobile
   hotspot from the Mobile hotspot menu.

2. To configure the following settings, press
   Configure:

- Network name: Change the moniker of your
  mobile hotspot.

- Password: Choosing a security level that
  requires a password grants access to or the
  ability to modify the information.

- The Band: Choose one of the available
  bandwidth alternatives.

- Security: Select mobile hotspot security levels.

- Advanced: Customize additional mobile
  hotspot configurations.

Auto hotspot

Automatically share the connection of the hotspot
with another device that is registered into your
Samsung account.

1. In the Settings menu, select ![wifi icon] Connections, then Mobile hotspot & tethering, followed by Mobile hotspot.

2. Touch the Auto hotspot button and press ![toggle] to enable this function.

Tethering

Tethering allows you to distribute the Internet connection of one device to multiple devices. Options are contingent upon the service provider.

1. In the Settings menu, navigate to ![wifi icon] Connections and select Mobile hotspot & tethering.

2. Tap a selection:

- To enable Bluetooth tethering, touch the device to allow Bluetooth to share its Internet connection.

- Use a USB cable to link your computer to your device, and then activate USB connectivity.

- Utilize the Ethernet adapter to connect your computer to your device, and then press the Ethernet tethering button.

Ethernet

In the absence of wireless network connectivity, one may use an Ethernet cable to link the device in question to a nearby network.

1. Connect an Ethernet cable to the device.

2. Follow the on-screen instructions after selecting 🛜 Connections > More connection settings > Ethernet from the Settings menu.

Note: An adapter (which is not included) is required to connect Ethernet cables to the device in use.

Unlock the network

Access the lock status of the device's network and determine whether the device is qualified to be unlocked so that it can be used on other mobile networks. Options are contingent upon the service provider.

o In the Settings menu, navigate to 🛜 Connections > More connections settings >

Networks unlock to access the following options:

- The Network Lock Status: Determine the current network lock status of your device.

- Permanent unlock: So that you can utilize your device with the other service provider, seek permanent network unlock.

- Transient unblocking: Obtain a transient network unlocking solution in order to enable device usage with the alternative service provider.

Connected devices

Ensure mobile continuity between your device and other devices that are connected. Options are contingent upon the service provider.

- o In the Settings menu, select Connected devices to access the following features:

- Quick Share: Facilitates the effortless sharing of files and documents between your device and any user with a Samsung account.

160

- Bud Auto-Switch: Automatically transfer your Galaxy Buds from other devices to this device whenever you answer calls, make phone calls, or play media.

- Text and phone calls on a different device: You can initiate and receive phone calls and text messages using Galaxy devices that are connected to the Samsung account you have.

- Proceed with applications on an alternative device: Recommence from the previous location on Galaxy devices that are currently logged into their Samsung account.

- Establish a connection between your device and a Windows PC to obtain immediate access to the device's files, including photos, messages, and more.

- Multiple controls: Utilize the Galaxy Book's keyboard and cursor to operate this device and to transfer items back and forth.

- Smart Views: Display the device's display or stream video on a nearby television.

- Galaxy Wearable: Use the earbuds and watch from Samsung to pair your device.

- Connect your device to the ecosystem of extremely intelligent living solutions using SmartThings.

- Android Auto: Establish a connection between your device and the displays of compatible vehicles so that you may concentrate on the road ahead.

Vibration and Sound

The vibrations and audio used to indicate notifications, screen touches, and other interactions could be modified.

Sound Mode

It is possible to toggle the sound mode on your device without employing the volume controls.

- Within the Settings menu, navigate to Sounds & vibration and choose a mode:

- Audio: Employ the decibel levels, vibrations, and sounds configured in the Sounds settings to deliver notifications and alerts.

- Configure the device to vibrate in addition to chiming in the event of a phone call.

- Vibrate: Only use vibration for notification and alert purposes.

- Mute: Configure the device to produce no sound.

- Temporary muting allows you to set a time limit for when your device is muted.

Tip: When switching sound modes, use the sound mode's settings instead of the volume controls to preserve the customized sound levels.

Mute using gesture

Quickly silence sounds by either obscuring the display or inverting the device.

- o From the Settings menu, select Advanced features > touch motions & gestures. To enable touch , deactivate the device using the gestures and then touch again.

Vibration

You can regulate the timing and manner in which your device resonates.

1. In the Configuration menu, select Sounds & vibration.

2. Touch based customization options:

- Call vibration: For phone calls, choose from the preset vibration patterns.

- Vibrations for notifications: Choose from the predetermined vibration patterns for notifications.

- System vibration: Establish the vibration feedback and intensity for the following configuration options:

- Vibration intensity of the system: Modify vibration intensities by adjusting the slider.

- Contact interactions: When you hold down items on the screen or contact navigation keys, a vibration occurs.

- Dialing keypads: Set a vibration for the phone keypad whenever you dial numbers.

- The Samsung keyboard: When using Samsung keyboards, the screen vibrates.

- Charging: Produces a vibration upon connecting the charger.

- The Navigation gestures: When gestures are utilized, it vibrates.

- Camera feedback: Vibrates during zooming, altering shooting modes, and taking photographs, among other operations.

- The Vibration Intensity: By rotating sliders, you can adjust the vibration intensity for

notifications, phone calls, and touch
interactions.

Volume

Volume adjustments are available for media, calls,
ringtones, notifications, and system noises.

- ○ Tap Sounds & vibration in the Settings
  menu, then tap Volume and drag the sliders
  corresponding to each sound type.

Tip: As an alternative, the intensity buttons can be
employed to adjust the intensity. When activated, the
pop-up menu exhibits the current sound type and
decibel level. You can expand menus by touching
them, and you can modify the volumes of various
types of sounds by dragging the sliders that they
contain.

Using the media volume buttons

Assign the default functionality of the Volume
buttons to regulate the volumes of the media sounds
being played, rather than the volume of the currently
active sound.

1. Select Volume from the Sounds & vibrations menu in the Settings menu.

2. To activate the feature, press the Dolby Volume controls for media.

Media volume limit

Limit the utmost output of the Bluetooth speakers or headphones (which are not included) on your device.

1. Select Volume from the Sounds & vibrations menu in the Settings menu.

2. Select More options followed by Media volume limit.

3. Press to activate this feature.

- To establish the utmost output volumes, utilize the Custom Volumes Limit slider.

- To enable PIN authentication for volume adjustments, select Set volumes limit PIN.

Ringtone

You can modify the ringtone of a phone call by adding your own or selecting from the preset noises. Options are contingent upon the service provider.

1. Select Ringtone from the Sounds & vibrations menu in the Settings menu.

2. To adjust the volume of your ringtone, move the slider.

3. To select a ringtone from a preview, simply touch the desired tone; alternatively, to use audio files as ringtones, tap Add.

Notification sound

Preset sounds are available for selection in relation to each notification alert.

1. Select Notification's sound from the Sounds & vibrations menu in the Settings menu.

2. To adjust the volume of the notification ringtone, simply drag the slider.

3. To select a sound after hearing a preview, tap it.

Tip: Additionally, use the application's settings menu to personalize the noises of the notifications so that they are unique to each application.

App notifications

Define the applications that are granted permission to transmit notifications to you.

o To enable notifications for individual applications, navigate to Settings > 🔲 Notifications > Application notifications and then tap.

Lock screen notification

Determine which notifications are enabled to appear on the Lock screen.

o To enable the feature, navigate to Settings > 🔲 Notifications > Lock screen's notifications > Press. To modify settings, touch:

- Hide contents: Prevent the visibility of notifications in the Notification pane.

- Present information: Exhibit notifications within the Notification pane.

- Present contents when unlocked: exhibit notification contents in the absence of a locked screen.

- Displayed Notifications: Select which of the available notifications to exhibit on the Lock screen.

- Always-On-Display: Incorporate notifications into the Always-on-Display interface.

Notification popup style

You can modify the appearance and additional configurations of the notifications.

o Select the desired pop-up styles from the Notifications menu in the Settings menu by tapping Notifications > Notifications pop-up style.

- In summary: Enable the ability to personalize the notifications.

- Applications for brief notification display: Choose applications for brief notification display.

- Edge lighting styles: Choose the edge lighting design to display notifications.

- Color by keyword: Customize the appearance of notifications by including keywords that are particularly significant to you.

- Indicate notifications even when the screen is off: Select whether to indicate notifications even when the screen is off.

• Comprehensive: Enable the Samsung Notifications settings by default.

Do not disturb

This feature allows users to easily disable notifications and audio upon activating this mode. One could also designate exceptions for individuals, applications, and alarms. Additionally, it is possible to establish schedules for recurring events, such as meetings or sleep.

○ Navigate to Settings > Notifications > Do-not-disturb and configure the following:

• To enable the do-not-disturb feature, merely enable it to silence notifications and sounds.

- For what period of time?When manually activating Do-not-disturb mode, choose the default duration.

Schedule

- One can personalize schedules for the do-not-disturb mode during sleep.

- Adding schedule: Establish the days and times that your device should be placed in Do-not-disturb mode via new schedules.

- Permitted during do-not-disturb.

- Touch messages and phone calls to enable exceptions for Do-not-disturb.

- Application notifications: Enable notifications from specific applications during the do-not-disturb setting. Notifications of incoming messages, phone calls, and conversations would continue to reach you even if you disabled associated applications.

- Alarms and vibrations can be activated in conjunction with events, reminders, and alarms, provided that the do-not-disturb mode is still in effect.

- Disable notifications: Navigate to the customization options page to disable notifications.

Advanced notification settings

Notifications from services and applications could be configured.

o Select Advanced settings from the Notifications menu in the Settings menu.

- One can modify the quantity of notifications that are displayed on the Status indicator.

- Indicate battery percentage: Present the current battery life of your device in the status bars.

- Notification histories: Present snoozed notifications in addition to the most recent.

- Conversation notifications can be accessed via conversations. To configure the conversation's notification as silent, alerting, or as a priority, depress the button.

- Floating notifications: Enable floating notifications on the Smart pop-up view or the Bubbles view.

- Suggest actions and replies for notifications: Obtain pertinent recommendations for the actions to be taken in response to your notifications and replies to the messages.

- Enable the snooze button: When the button is activated, it can be used to quickly delay notifications.

- Notification reminders: Activate and personalize the recurring reminders that appear on notifications from selected services and applications. By clearing the notifications, the reminders will cease.

- Application icon badges: Indicate which applications feature badges that denote highly active notifications within their icons. By touching the badges, one can determine whether or not they display the quantities of unread notifications.

- Wireless Emergency Alert: Tailor your alert notifications to reflect your preferences.

Notify when the call is connected

It is possible to program your device to vibrate whenever you take up the phone as an alert for missed calls and messages.

To enable this feature, navigate to Settings > Advanced features > touch gestures & motions > then Alert when the smartphone is lifted up.

Display

You could configure the font size, screen brightness, termination delay, and numerous other display settings.

Dark mode

This feature allows you to switch to a darker theme, which dims the white/bright screens and notifications, to provide enhanced visual comfort during the night.

- o Select Display from the Settings menu to access the following options:

- Light: Apply a theme of any light color to the device (the default).

- Dark: Simply imbue the device with any dark color scheme.

- Dark mode configuration: Personalize the location and timing of the Dark mode activation.

  – To activate dark modes, configure them for the Sunset-to-sunrise or Custom schedules.

Screen brightness

Screen brightness can be modified in accordance with individual preference or illumination circumstances.

1. In the Settings menu, select Display.

2. Modify the following settings within Brightness:

- To establish custom brightness levels, adjust the Brightness sliders.

- Select Adaptive brightness to have the screen's luminance modified automatically in response to the surrounding lighting conditions.

- Additionally, the screen luminance can be easily modified through the Quick settings pane.

Smoothness of movement

Obtain more fluid navigation and authentic-looking animations by simply increasing your screen's refresh rate.

1. In the Settings menu, navigate to Display > Motion fluidity.

2. After selecting an option, tap Apply.

Eye comfort shield

The functionality has the potential to improve sleep quality and reduce eye strain. You could programmatically turn this feature on and off according to your preferences.

1. In the Settings menu, navigate to Display > Eyes comfort shield, and then press to activate this function.

2. Touch the customization option:

- Adaptive to automatically adjust the color temperature of your screen based on your usage patterns and the precise time of day.

- Capable of configuring a schedule for the activation of eye comfort shields at any time.

- In the Set schedule menu, choose Custom, Sunset-to-sunrise, or Always on.

- Adjust the color temperature sliders in order to configure the opacity of the filter.

Screen mode

The device features a variety of screen mode options that alter the quality of the display to suit the circumstances. The mode could be selected according to personal preference.

1. In the Settings menu, navigate to Display > Screen mode.

2. Select the option to configure an additional screen mode.

- In order to modify the white balance, slide the slider.

- To manually modify RGB values, navigate to the Advanced settings menu.

Font style and size

You could modify the font size and style in order to easily personalize your device.

- o In the Settings menu, select Display > Font size & style to access the following options:
- Simply press the Font style button to change the font.
- – To select a font, simply touch it, or alternatively, tap Download font to import fonts directly from the Galaxy Store.
- By touching Bold fonts, the bold weight of each font will be displayed.
- To modify the size of the text, utilize the font size sliders.

Screen zoom

The levels of zooming can be adjusted to make the content more legible.

1. Navigate to Settings > Display > Screen zoom.

2. Modify the zoom levels by adjusting the screen's zoom sliders.

Full screen application

The selection of applications to be utilized is contingent upon the aspect ratio of the full-screen display.

o To enable this function and modify its settings, navigate to Display > Full screen applications from the Settings menu. From there, select Applications.

Camera cutout

With a black bar, you can conceal the camera cutout region.

o In the Settings menu, navigate to Display > Camera cutout and select Applications to enable this function and modify its settings.

Screen timeout

The screen can be programmed to turn off at the specified time.

o Within the Settings menu, navigate to Display > Screen timeout and tap a time limit to configure it.

Note: Prolonged exposure to static images, excluding Always-On-Display modes, may result in image degradation or a permanent ghost-like afterimage.

Turn off the display screen when not in use.

Prevent accidental contact

Prevent the display from detecting touch input when the device is in a dark location, such as a pocket or bag.

o Press Display > Accidental touch protections from the Settings menu to enable the features.

Touch sensitivity

It is possible to increase the touch sensitivity of a screen in order to utilize screen protectors.

o Simply navigate to Settings > Display > Touch sensitivity to activate it.

Display charging information

The battery level and an estimated time remaining until the device is fully charged may be exhibited when the screen is in the off position.

- To activate, navigate to Settings > Display > Show charging information.

Screen saver

It is possible to observe photographs or colors even when the screen is off or while it is charging.

1. Select Screen saver from the Display menu in the Settings menu.

2. Choose one of the following options:

- None: No screen saver is displayed.

- Colours: To display the changing colour screens, tap your selector.

- Photo tables: Utilize photograph tables to exhibit images.

- Photograph frame: Utilize a photograph frame to exhibit images.

- Photos: Display images currently stored in your Google Photos account.

3. To view a demonstration of the selected screen saver, click Preview.

Tip: For additional options, touch Settings close to the feature.

List to wake
To activate the screen, simply raise the device.

o To enable this function, navigate to Settings > Advanced features > Motions & gestures > Lift-to-wake.

Double tap to wake up screen
Instead of using the Side key, simply double-tap to activate the display.

o To activate this feature, navigate to Settings > Advanced features > Motions & gestures > Double-tap the switch to turn it on.

Double tap to turn off screen
You can disable your device's display by double-tapping instead of using the Side key.

o To enable this feature, navigate to Settings > Advanced features > Motions & gestures > double-tap while the screen is off.

Keep the screen on during playback

Utilize front-facing cameras to detect when you are staring at your screen in order to maintain its illumination.

o From the Settings, press Advanced features > touch Motions & gestures > then Keep your screen on when viewing, and touch to turn on the feature.

One hand mode

It was possible to modify the screen's configuration in order to enable one-handed operation of the device.

1. In the Settings menu, navigate to Advanced features, followed by One-handed mode.

2. Toggle the feature on, touch and select one of the following options:

• Motion: Perform a downward swipe in the center of the screen's base edge.

• Button: To reduce the scale of the display, press Home twice in rapid succession.

Security and lock screen

One potential measure to safeguard one's device and information is to configure the screen protection.

Type of screen lock

You may select from the following screen lock types that offer medium, high, or no security: swipe, PIN, pattern, password, or none.

Note: A biometric safeguard is also available to protect access to the device and any sensitive data contained within it.

Set up a secure screen lock

It is recommended that you install a secure screen lock (PIN, Password, or Pattern) on your device. In order to configure and activate the biometric locking, this is required.

1. Under Settings, navigate to Lock screen > Screens lock type > Screens lock, and then tap the secure screen lock (pattern, PIN, or password).

2. Press to enable the display of notifications on the lock screen. The subsequent choices are accessible:

- Hide contents: Prevent the Notification pane from displaying notifications.

- Display notifications in the Notification pane to display content.

- Present contents when unlocked: Indicate notification contents in the absence of a locked screen.

- Displayed Notifications: Select which of the available notifications to exhibit on the Lock screen.

- Always-On-Display Display: Incorporate notifications into the Always-on-Display interface.

3. To dismiss the menu, type Done.

4. Configure the subsequent screen lock options:

- The Smart Lock: Your device can be automatically unlocked upon detecting trustworthy locations or other devices. The safeguard on a secure screen is required for this feature.

- Secure lock configuration: Personalize the secure lock configuration. The safeguard on the secure screen is required for this feature.

- Lock screens: Modify the contents and visual design of your lock screen with a touch.

- The Widgets: To modify the widgets that appear alongside a clock on the Lock screen, tap.

- Select whether to permit modifications to the elements displayed on your Lock screens by holding them down while editing.

- Always-On-Display: Enable the screen that is constantly displayed.

- The Roaming Clock: While roaming, the time will be displayed both at your current location and at home.

- Concerning Lock screens: Lock screen software should be updated.

Chapter Five
Troubleshooting Tips

You may check for software updates and, if necessary, reset the device's services.

System updates or software updates

Locate and install the available software updates that correspond to the device in use. Options are dependent on the provider of the service.

- o To access the following options, select Software update or System update from the Settings menu:

- Maintain an eye out for updates: Manually check for software updates.

- Verify software updates: Perform a manual check for software updates.

- Maintain the update: Continue with the interrupted dispatches.

- Display the history of software updates: Access a comprehensive list of all software updates installed on your device.

- The Smart revisions: Configure automatic installation of security updates.

- Downloading and installing: When software updates become available, proceed with the installation process.

- Wi-Fi automatic transfer capabilities: Automatic software updates are downloaded whenever the device is connected to a Wi-Fi network.

- Acquire information regarding the installation process of your existing software.

- One should use software upgrade assistants: Utilize the Install tool to install system updates easily.

Reset to default

Reset both the device and the network configuration. Additionally, you can reset your device to factory settings.

Reset all settings

It is possible to reset your device to its factory settings, which deletes all data except for your security, account, and language configurations. No personal information is compromised.

1. In the Settings menu, navigate to ⚙ General management > select Reset > then Reset each configuration.

2. When prompted, press Reset settings and confirm.

Reset network settings

With the Reset networks settings option, it is possible to reset Wi-Fi, Bluetooth, and mobile data settings.

1. Click ⚙ General management from the Settings menu, and then tap Reset, followed by Reset networks settings.

2. When prompted, press Reset settings and confirm.

Reset accessibility settings

The accessibility settings of a device can be reset. Personal information and downloaded application accessibility settings remain unaffected.

1. Click General management > Reset > Reset accessibility settings from the Settings menu.

2. When prompted, press Reset settings and confirm.

Restore factory data

You have the ability to reset the device to its factory settings, which will delete all data.

This operation deletes ALL data from your device, including settings for Google and other accounts, app and system data, downloaded applications, photographs, music, videos, and other files. The information stored on the external SD device remains unaltered.

As soon as you set the Lock screen and log in to your Google Account on your device, Google Devices Protection is activated automatically.

Note: It may take up to twenty-four hours for the re-encrypted Google Account password to synchronize with all devices associated with that account.

Before resetting the device:

1. Verify that the desired files have been transferred to the designated storage location.

2. Log in to your Google Account and validate your password and username.

In order to reset devices:

1. In the Settings menu, select General administration > Reset > Factory data reset.

2. Command "Reset" and adhere to the on-screen instructions to initiate the reset process.

3. Following a device restart, adhere to the necessary configuration prompts.